HEALING VERSES
OF THE
Psalms

COMPILED BY DR. STEVE VENTOLA

STATURE PUBLICATIONS

STATURE PUBLICATIONS

Ventola, Steve, Healing Verses of the Psalms.
Copyright information available upon request.

Library of Congress Control Number:
ISBN 13: 978-0-9829598-0-0
ISBN 10: 0-9829598-0-X

Cover Design: Copen Marketing & Design
Illustrations: Robert Kauffman
Interior Design: J. L. Saloff
Fonts: Garamond Premier Pro, Minion Pro

All verses are from the King James Version of the Bible.

Published in the United States of America on acid-free paper.
First Edition: v. 1.0

This compilation is dedicated to all those who have kept and are keeping their integrity and uprightness which upholds us all.

Appreciation

As it seems right to give thanks and praise, I would offer a special thank you to Deborah Rhodes for her ready agreement and insightful suggestions, as well as her expert editing skills, and to Robert Kauffman for his beautiful illustrations. I would like to acknowledge my parents, Samuel and Josephine Ventola, for all they provided for me while they lived. Thank you also to Carol Smith, my brother Dr. Joseph Ventola, and my sisters Linda and Lori, for their unending support and love, as well as all other family, friends and patients who have provided encouragement in this project. And, lastly, a depth of gratitude to all the spiritual educators I have had who have led me in the way of truly appreciating the Book of Psalms and its healing words.

Introduction

Surely there are many verses of the psalms that can be considered to be of a healing nature. For those who, like myself, may have a love of the psalms, I have selected verses from the King James Version of the Bible that seem to me to offer a particular healing quality. This process was a labor of love, the fruits of which I share with you today, trusting that the words contained herein will serve to draw you into an experience where all is well. Let

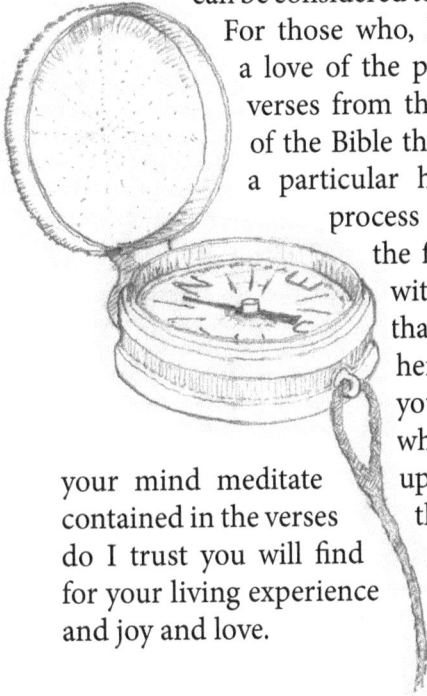

your mind meditate upon the spiritual gold contained in the verses that strike you. As you do I trust you will find the answers required for your living experience to be filled with peace and joy and love.

Suggestions for Use

Read until you find the verse wherein your heart comes to rest, where you experience an infilling of relaxation and release of tension, a sense of upliftment in place of devastation or illness, joy instead of sadness, peace replacing conflict, perhaps even an inclination to forgive, or a sense of thankfulness for the blessings received. You may wish to put that verse on paper and review it in the evening and morning. You could carry it with you during the day and refer to it as needed for strength in times of need, or for greater life enhancement. You may also find that writing down some of your meditations regarding the verse may help you to find a deeper knowing and appreciation of the spirit contained therein. Additionally, for greater understanding and clarity, I would encourage you to read the "Insights" that are included with some of the verses.

My wish is that this compilation of healing verses may serve as a means for you to be victorious in life, a means whereby you may wax strong in grace and stature so that you may be a blessing to others in all the days of your living.

Dr. Steve Ventola

HEALING VERSES
OF THE
Psalms

COMPILED BY DR. STEVE VENTOLA

Blessed is *the man that walketh not in the counsel of the ungodly, nor standeth in the way of sinners, nor sitteth in the seat of the scornful.*

But his delight is *in the law of the LORD; and in his law doth he meditate day and night.*

PSALM 1

But thou, O LORD, art *a shield for me, my glory and the lifter up of mine head.*

I laid me down and slept; I awaked; for the LORD sustained me.

Salvation belongeth *unto the LORD: thy blessing* is *upon thy people. Selah[1].*

PSALM 3

INSIGHT: 1) According to several sources, "*Selah*" is a "term of unknown meaning..." Some suggest a variety of musical directions (since originally the psalms were sung, accompanied by musical instruments), earlier traditions thought it meant "for ever." I sense that it is a sacred word, similar in purpose to Amen.

Stand in awe, and sin not: commune with your own heart upon your bed, and be still. Selah.

Offer the sacrifices of righteousness, and put your trust in the LORD.

LORD, lift thou up the light of thy countenance upon us.

Thou hast put gladness in my heart, more than in the time that *their corn and their wine increased.*

I will both lay me down in peace, and sleep: for thou, LORD, only makest me dwell in safety.

PSALM 4

My voice shalt thou hear in the morning, O LORD; in the morning will I direct my prayer unto thee, and will look up.

But as for me, I will come into thy house in the multitude of thy mercy: and in thy fear² will I worship toward thy holy temple.

But let all those that put their trust in thee rejoice: let them ever shout for joy, because thou defendest them: let them also that love thy name be joyful in thee.

PSALM 5

INSIGHT: 2) "Strong's Hebrew and Greek Dictionaries" note that the word 'fear' can also be translated as 'reverence'.

Depart from me, all ye workers of iniquity; for the LORD hath heard the voice of my weeping[3].

The LORD hath heard my supplication; the LORD will receive my prayer.

PSALM 6

INSIGHT: 3) One of the definitions of the word *"weeping"* in "Merriam Webster's Collegiate Dictionary" is "To express passion by shedding tears." To my mind, this relates to a passion to invite the Lord to come into our hearts and minds. When that passion is such that we are "moved to tears," there is an answer, reflected in the next verse, where one of the definitions of the word 'supplication,' according to "Strong's Hebrew and Greek Dictionaries," is 'graciousness.' The Lord is gracious, and as we invite Him truly, purely and passionately into our hearts and minds, He *"will receive"* our *"prayer,"* that is, our invitation, and us.

O LORD my God, in thee do I put my trust.

Awake for me to[4] *the judgment* that *thou hast commanded.*

The LORD shall judge the people: judge me, O LORD, according to my righteousness, and according to mine integrity...

The righteous God trieth the hearts and reins.

I will praise the LORD according to his righteousness: and will sing praise to the name of the LORD most high.

PSALM 7

INSIGHT: 4) In the KJV, certain words that were not in the original Hebrew and Greek text were added by the translators, who felt they were necessary for clarity in English. In the Bible, the added words are in italics, but in our compilation they are not italicized, such as the words "to" and "that" in this verse. In a few instances, we have found that a verse has more impact without the added words. Try rereading this verse without them. You may also wish to explore reading other verses without them.

O LORD our Lord, how excellent is thy name in all the earth! who hast set thy glory above the heavens.

Out of the mouth of babes and sucklings hast thou ordained strength because of thine enemies, that thou mightest still the enemy and the avenger.

What is man, that thou art mindful of him?

For thou hast made him a little lower than the angels, and hast crowned him with glory and honour.

Thou madest him to have dominion over the works of thy hands; thou hast put all things under his feet:

All sheep and oxen, yea, and the beasts of the field;[5]

The fowl of the air, and the fish of the sea, and whatsoever *passeth through the paths of the seas*[6].

O LORD our Lord, how excellent is thy name in all the earth!

PSALM 8

INSIGHT: 5) Some allegorical symbolism could suggest that "*sheep*" is a metaphor for the faithful, or those who are true to the Truth they know; "*oxen*" could symbolize the stubborn human mind, while the "*beasts of the field*" could be seen as analogous to destructive emotions such as jealousy, hate, disdain. 6) Likewise, the "*fowl of the air*" could symbolize conscious thoughts of a higher or spiritual nature, while "*fish*" and "whatsoever *passeth through the paths of the seas*" could relate to the subconscious or unconscious.

Thou madest him to have dominion...

When mine enemies[7] are turned back, they shall fall and perish at thy presence.

Thou hast destroyed the wicked, thou hast put out their name for ever and ever.

He shall minister judgment to the people in uprightness.

And they that know thy name will put their trust in thee: for thou, LORD, hast not forsaken them that seek thee.

Sing praises to the LORD, which dwelleth in Zion: declare among the people his doings.

He forgetteth not the cry of the humble.

Thou that liftest me up from the gates of death:

That I may shew forth all thy praise in the gates of the daughter of Zion: I will rejoice in thy salvation.

PSALM 9

INSIGHT: 7) In my meditations, *"enemies"* don't always refer to individuals, neighbors, coworkers, government, peoples or nations. Quite often our worst enemies are the attitudes we take toward ourselves and others, attitudes such as accusation, blame, criticism, contempt, impatience, low self-esteem, gossip, laziness, victimization, jealousy and hatred. These enemies do perish in the Presence of the Lord.

The LORD is King for ever and ever: the heathen are perished out of his land.

LORD, thou hast heard the desire of the humble: thou wilt prepare their heart, thou wilt cause thine ear to hear:

To judge the fatherless and the oppressed, that the man of the earth may no more oppress.

PSALM 10

In the LORD put I my trust...

The LORD is in his holy temple, the LORD'S throne is in heaven...

For the righteous LORD loveth righteousness; his countenance doth behold the upright.

PSALM 11

The words of the LORD are *pure words*: as *silver tried in a furnace of earth, purified seven times.*

Thou shalt keep them, O LORD, thou shalt preserve them from this generation for ever.

PSALM 12

I have trusted in thy mercy; my heart shall rejoice in thy salvation.

I will sing unto the LORD, because he hath dealt bountifully with me.

PSALM 13

LORD, who shall abide in thy tabernacle? who shall dwell in thy holy hill?

He that *walketh uprightly, and worketh righteousness, and speaketh the truth in his heart.*

He that *backbiteth not with his tongue, nor doeth evil to his neighbour, nor taketh up a reproach against his neighbour.*

He honoureth them that fear[8] the LORD...

He ... *putteth not out his money to usury, nor taketh reward against the innocent. He that doeth these* things *shall never be moved.*

PSALM 15

INSIGHT: 8) Not *"fear"* as in being afraid of, but fear as in reverence, respect.

11

A Golden Psalm[9]

Preserve me, O God: for in thee do I put my trust.

The lines are fallen unto me in pleasant places; *yea, I have a goodly heritage.*

I will bless the LORD, who hath given me counsel: my reins also instruct me in the night seasons.

I have set the LORD always before me: because he is *at my right hand, I shall not be moved.*

Therefore my heart is glad, and my glory rejoiceth: my flesh also shall rest in hope.[10]

Neither wilt thou suffer thine Holy One to see corruption.

Thou wilt shew me the path of life: in thy presence is *fulness of joy; at thy right hand* there are *pleasures for evermore.*

PSALM 16

INSIGHT: 9) Psalm 16 is subtitled "A Michtam of David." Although a few meanings have been suggested, such as 'contemplation' and 'song,' the derivation of the word "Michtam" is obscure. In "The Holy Bible Old and New Testaments, King James Version," 1972, by Thomas Nelson Inc., a study Bible, there is this alternate translation noted in the center-column references: "Or a golden psalm." Since gold can be symbolic of God's Love, it seemed appropriate to retain that spirit in the title of this psalm. 10) Try substituting the word 'confidence' for the word 'hope' here, so it reads *my flesh also shall rest in* confidence." In my perception, the reality of hope is based in confidence in the ways and the laws of God, in which, as it is put in the first verse, *"do I put my trust."*

Let my sentence come forth from thy presence...

Hold up my goings in thy paths, that *my footsteps slip not.*

Keep me as the apple of the eye, hide me under the shadow of thy wings,

As for me, I will behold thy face in righteousness: I shall be satisfied, when I awake, with thy likeness.

PSALM 17

Hold up my goings in thy paths...

I will love thee, O LORD, my strength.

The LORD is my rock, and my fortress, and my deliverer; my God, my strength, in whom I will trust; my buckler, and the horn of my salvation...

He heard my voice out of his temple,

He sent from above, he took me, he drew me out of many waters.

The LORD was my stay.

He brought me forth also into a large place; he delivered me, because he delighted in me.

I was also upright before him, and I kept myself from mine iniquity.

With the merciful thou wilt shew thyself merciful; with an upright man thou wilt shew thyself upright;

With the pure thou wilt shew thyself pure...

For thou wilt light my candle: the LORD my God will enlighten my darkness.

By my God have I leaped over a wall.

As for *God, his way is perfect ... a buckler[11] to all those that trust in him.*

It is *God that girdeth me with strength, and maketh my way perfect.*

He ... setteth me upon my high places.

Thou hast also given me the shield of thy salvation: and thy right hand hath holden me up, and thy gentleness hath made me great.

Thou hast enlarged my steps under me, that my feet did not slip.

Thou hast delivered me from the strivings of the people...

Let the God of my salvation be exalted.

Therefore will I give thanks unto thee, O LORD, among the heathen, and sing praises unto thy name.

PSALM 18

INSIGHT: 11) A *"buckler"* was a small rounded shield carried in the hand or worn on the arm, perhaps symbolizing protection in all aspects of one's being, above down and inside out, from the smallest to the largest, from the invisible to the visible. This protection comes to and through each one who puts full trust in the Lord.

The law of the LORD is perfect, converting the soul: the testimony of the LORD is sure, making wise the simple.

The statutes of the LORD are right, rejoicing the heart: the commandment of the LORD is pure, enlightening the eyes.

The fear of the LORD is clean, enduring for ever: the judgments of the LORD are true and righteous altogether.

More to be desired are they[12] *than gold, yea, than much fine gold: sweeter also than honey and the honeycomb.*

INSIGHT: 12) Here is another instance where the verse seems clearer without the added, unitalicized words. Try reading it without them.

Moreover by them is thy servant warned: and *in keeping of them* there is *great reward.*

Who can understand his *errors? cleanse thou me from secret* faults.

Keep back thy servant also from presumptuous sins; *let them not have dominion over me: then shall I be upright, and I shall be innocent from the great transgression.*

Let the words of my mouth, and the meditation of my heart, be acceptable in thy sight, O LORD, my strength, and my redeemer.

PSALM 19

The LORD hear thee in the day of trouble...

Send thee help from the sanctuary, and strengthen thee...

Grant thee according to thine own heart, and fulfil all thy counsel.

Now know I that the LORD saveth his anointed; he will hear him from his holy heaven with the saving strength of his right hand.

We are risen, and stand upright.

PSALM *20*

They cried unto thee, and were delivered: they trusted in thee, and were not confounded.

Save me from the lion's mouth: for thou hast heard me from the horns of the unicorns.

I will declare thy name unto my brethren: in the midst of the congregation will I praise thee.

Ye that fear[13] the LORD, praise him ... glorify him; and fear him...

All the ends of the world shall remember and turn unto the LORD: and all the kindreds of the nations shall worship before thee.

For the kingdom is the LORD'S: and he is the governor among the nations.

And none can keep alive his own soul.

PSALM *22*

INSIGHT: 13) Again, *"fear"* in the sense of honor and respect, not fearful or afraid.

The LORD is my shepherd; I shall not want.

He maketh me to lie down in green pastures: he leadeth me beside the still waters.

He restoreth my soul: he leadeth me in the paths of righteousness for his name's sake.

Yea, though I walk through the valley of the shadow of death,[14] I will fear no evil: for thou art with me; thy rod and thy staff they comfort me.

Thou preparest a table before me in the presence of mine enemies:[15] thou anointest my head with oil; my cup runneth over.

Surely goodness and mercy shall follow me all the days of my life: and I will dwell in the house of the LORD for ever.

PSALM *23*

INSIGHT: 14) In thinking about what "*the valley of the shadow of death*" might relate to, it occurred to me that originally, man was created to live, and not die. According to Genesis, dying was the result only when human beings disobeyed the Lord's one command not to eat of the fruit of the tree of the knowledge of good and evil. Thus, "*the valley of the shadow of death*" could symbolize the world as it has become, a state where human beings have disconnected themselves from God and the Garden that was originally created. "*The valley of the shadow of death,*" something we walk through every day of our lives in man's present state of consciousness, but not something that was ever intended to be. 15) As previously noted, sometimes one's enemies are that which are closest to one, such as negative thoughts and feelings about oneself or others.

Who shall ascend into the hill of the LORD? or who shall stand in his holy place?

He that hath clean hands, and a pure heart; who hath not lifted up his soul unto vanity, nor sworn deceitfully.

He shall receive the blessing from the LORD, and righteousness from the God of his salvation.

Lift up your heads, O ye gates; and be ye lift up, ye everlasting doors; and the King of glory shall come in.

Who is this King of glory? The LORD strong and mighty, the LORD mighty in battle.

The LORD of hosts, he is the King of glory. Selah.

PSALM *24*

Unto thee, O LORD, do I lift up my soul.

Yea, let none that wait on thee be ashamed...

Lead me in thy truth, and teach me: for thou art *the God of my salvation; on thee do I wait all the day.*

What man is *he that feareth the LORD? him shall he teach in the way* that *he shall choose.*

His soul shall dwell at ease; and his seed shall inherit the earth.

The secret of the LORD is *with them that fear him; and he will shew them his covenant.*

Mine eyes are *ever toward the LORD; for he shall pluck my feet out of the net.*

Look upon mine affliction and my pain; and forgive all my sins.

Let integrity and uprightness preserve me; for I wait on thee.

PSALM 25

Judge me, O LORD; for I have walked in mine integrity: I have trusted also in the LORD; therefore I shall not slide.

Examine me, O LORD, and prove me; try my reins and my heart.

For thy lovingkindness is before mine eyes: and I have walked in thy truth.

I will wash mine hands in innocency: so will I compass thine altar, O LORD:

That I may publish with the voice of thanksgiving, and tell of all thy wondrous works.

LORD, I have loved the habitation of thy house, and the place where thine honour dwelleth.

My foot standeth in an even place: in the congregations will I bless the LORD.

PSALM 26

The LORD is my light and my salvation; whom shall I fear? the LORD is the strength of my life; of whom shall I be afraid?

One thing have I desired of the LORD ... that I may dwell in the house of the LORD all the days of my life, to behold the beauty of the LORD, and to enquire in his temple.

And now shall mine head be lifted up ... therefore will I offer in his tabernacle sacrifices of joy; I will sing, yea, I will sing praises unto the LORD.

...Thy face, LORD, will I seek.

Thou hast been my help ... O God of my salvation.

Wait on the LORD: be of good courage, and he shall strengthen thine heart: wait, I say, on the LORD.

PSALM 27

I lift up my hands toward thy holy oracle.[16]

The LORD is *my strength and my shield; my heart trusted in him, and I am helped: therefore my heart greatly rejoiceth; and with my song will I praise him.*

The LORD ... is *the saving strength of his anointed.*

PSALM 28

Worship the LORD in the beauty of holiness.

The voice of the LORD is *powerful; the voice of the LORD* is *full of majesty.*

And in his temple doth every one speak of his glory.

The LORD will give strength unto his people; the LORD will bless his people with peace.

PSALM 29

INSIGHT: 16) In the days when the psalms were written, an *"oracle"* was considered a conveyance of words of wisdom. "The Holman Bible Dictionary" indicates that the word for 'oracle' can also be translated as "communication with God," or 'saying,' 'burden' and 'word.' "Strong's Concordance" indicates that 'oracle' could refer to "the innermost part of the Sanctuary," or the most holy place, whereas "Easton's Dictionary" indicates 'oracle' can also refer to the "Word of God." We could consider *"oracle"* here as "Word." "*I lift up my hands toward thy holy* Word."

O LORD my God, I cried unto thee, and thou hast healed me.

O LORD, thou hast brought up my soul from the grave: thou hast kept me alive, that I should not go down to the pit.

Sing unto the LORD, O ye saints of his, and give thanks at the remembrance of his holiness.

Weeping may endure for a night, but joy cometh in the morning.

Thou hast turned for me my mourning into dancing: thou hast put off my sackcloth, and girded me with gladness;

To the end that my glory may sing praise to thee, and not be silent. O LORD my God, I will give thanks unto thee for ever.

PSALM 30

Let me not be ashamed, O LORD; for I have called upon thee...

Oh how great is thy goodness, which thou hast laid up for them that fear thee; which thou hast wrought for them that trust in thee before the sons of men!

Thou shalt hide them in the secret of thy presence from the pride of man: thou shalt keep them secretly in a pavilion from the strife of tongues.

For I said in my haste, I am cut off from before thine eyes: nevertheless thou heardest the voice of my supplications when I cried unto thee.

O love the LORD, all ye his saints: for the LORD preserveth the faithful, and plentifully rewardeth the proud doer.

Be of good courage, and he shall strengthen your heart, all ye that hope in the LORD.

PSALM 31

Blessed is *the man unto whom the LORD imputeth not iniquity, and in whose spirit* there is *no guile.*

He that trusteth in the LORD, mercy shall compass him about.

Be glad in the LORD, and rejoice, ye righteous: and shout for joy, all ye that are *upright in heart.*

PSALM 32

Behold, the eye of the LORD is upon them that fear him, upon them that hope in his mercy;

To deliver their soul from death, and to keep them alive in famine.

Let thy mercy, O LORD, be upon us, according as we hope in thee.

PSALM 33

I sought the LORD, and he heard me, and delivered me from all my fears.

They looked unto him, and were lightened: and their faces were not ashamed.

The angel of the LORD encampeth round about them that fear him, and delivereth them.

O fear[17] the LORD, ye his saints: for there is no want to them that fear[18] him.

Keep thy tongue from evil, and thy lips from speaking guile.

Depart from evil, and do good; seek peace, and pursue it.

The LORD is nigh unto them that are of a broken heart; and saveth such as be of a contrite spirit.

Many are the afflictions of the righteous: but the LORD delivereth him out of them all.

The LORD redeemeth the soul of his servants: and none of them that trust in him shall be desolate.

PSALM 34

INSIGHT: 17) Try the word 'honor' here. 18) Try substituting the word 'reverence' or 'respect' here.

Say unto my soul, I am thy salvation.

Let the LORD be magnified, which hath pleasure in the prosperity of his servant.

PSALM 35

Thy mercy, O LORD, is in the heavens; and thy faithfulness reacheth unto the clouds.

How excellent is thy lovingkindness, O God! therefore the children of men put their trust under the shadow of thy wings.

Thou shalt make them drink of the river of thy pleasures.

For with thee is the fountain of life: in thy light shall we see light.

O continue thy lovingkindness unto them that know thee; and thy righteousness to the upright in heart.

Let not the foot of pride come against me, and let not the hand of the wicked remove me.

PSALM 36

Trust in the LORD, and do good; so shalt thou dwell in the land, and verily thou shalt be fed.

Delight thyself also in the LORD; and he shall give thee the desires of thine heart.

Commit thy way unto the LORD; trust also in him; and he shall bring it to pass.

Rest in the LORD, and wait patiently for him: fret not...

Cease from anger, and forsake wrath: fret not thyself in any wise to do evil.

But the meek shall inherit the earth; and shall delight themselves in the abundance of peace.

They shall not be ashamed in the evil time: and in the days of famine they shall be satisfied.

The steps of a good[19] *man are ordered by the LORD: and he delighteth in his way.*

Though he fall, he shall not be utterly cast down: for the LORD upholdeth him with *his hand.*

The law of his God is in his heart; none of his steps shall slide.

Mark the perfect man, *and behold hold the upright: for the end of* that *man is peace.*

And the LORD shall help them ... and save them, because they trust in him.

INSIGHT: 19) Try reading this verse without the un-italicized, added word "good." It occurs to me that the steps of all men (and women), good, bad or indifferent, could be *"ordered"* (that is, prepared, provided for, or confirmed) by the Lord. A person just needs to listen for what those steps are, and take them one by one.

Mine iniquities are gone over mine head: as an heavy burden they are too heavy for me.

For in thee, O LORD, do I hope: thou wilt hear, O Lord my God.

For I am *ready to halt, and my sorrow* is *continually* before me.

PSALM 38

And now, Lord, what wait I for? my hope is in thee.

Deliver me from all my transgressions: make me not the reproach of the foolish.

O spare me, that I may recover strength, before I go hence, and be no more.

PSALM 39

For I am ready to halt...
...my hope is in thee.

I waited patiently for the LORD; and he inclined unto me, and heard my cry.

He brought me up also out of an horrible pit, out of the miry clay, and set my feet upon a rock, and established my goings.

And he hath put a new song in my mouth, even praise unto our God: many shall see it, and fear, and shall trust in the LORD.

Blessed is that man that maketh the LORD his trust, and respecteth not the proud, nor such as turn aside to lies.

Sacrifice and offering thou didst not desire; mine ears hast thou opened: burnt offering and sin offering hast thou not required.

I delight to do thy will, O my God: yea, thy law is within my heart.

I have not hid thy righteousness within my heart; I have declared thy faithfulness and thy salvation: I have not concealed thy lovingkindness and thy truth from the great congregation.

Let thy lovingkindness and thy truth continually preserve me.

Let all those that seek thee rejoice and be glad in thee: let such as love thy salvation say continually, The LORD be magnified.

PSALM 40

Blessed is he that considereth the poor: the LORD will deliver him in time of trouble.

The LORD will strengthen him upon the bed of languishing...

I said, LORD, be merciful unto me: heal my soul; for I have sinned against thee.

But thou, O LORD, be merciful unto me, and raise me up...

...thou upholdest me in mine integrity, and settest me before thy face for ever.

PSALM 41

As the hart panteth after the water brooks, so panteth my soul after thee, O God.

My soul thirsteth for God, for the living God...

Why art thou cast down, O my soul? and why art thou disquieted in me? hope thou in God: for I shall yet praise him for the help of his countenance.

O my God, my soul is cast down within me: therefore will I remember thee...

Yet the LORD will command his lovingkindness in the daytime, and in the night his song shall be with me, and my prayer unto the God of my life.

PSALM 42

O send out thy light and thy truth: let them lead me; let them bring me unto thy holy hill, and to thy tabernacles.

Then will I go unto the altar of God, unto God my exceeding joy: yea, upon the harp will I praise thee, O God my God.

Why art thou cast down, O my soul? and why art thou disquieted within me? hope in God: for I shall yet praise him, who is *the health of my countenance, and my God.*

PSALM 43

Thou art my King, O God...

In God we boast all the day long, and praise thy name for ever. Selah.

Our heart is not turned back, neither have our steps declined from thy way;

If we have forgotten the name of our God, or stretched out our hands to a strange god;

Shall not God search this out? for he knoweth the secrets of the heart.

Arise for our help, and redeem us for thy mercies' sake.

PSALM 44

My heart is inditing a good matter ... my tongue is the pen of a ready writer.

And in thy majesty ride prosperously because of truth and meekness and righteousness...

Thy throne, O God, is for ever and ever: the sceptre of thy kingdom is a right sceptre.

God, thy God, hath anointed thee with the oil of gladness above thy fellows.

All thy garments smell of myrrh, and aloes, and cassia, out of the ivory palaces, whereby they have made thee glad.

I will make thy name to be remembered in all generations: therefore shall the people praise thee for ever and ever.

PSALM 45

42

God is our refuge and strength, a very present help in trouble.

Therefore will not we fear, though the earth be removed, and though the mountains be carried into the midst of the sea;

There is a river, the streams whereof shall make glad the city of God, the holy place of the tabernacles of the most High.

God is in the midst of her; she shall not be moved: God shall help her, and that right early.

The LORD of hosts is with us; the God of Jacob is our refuge. Selah.

PSALM 46

O clap your hands, all ye people; shout unto God with the voice of triumph.

He shall choose our inheritance for us, the excellency of Jacob whom he loved. Selah.

God is gone up with a shout, the LORD with the sound of a trumpet.

Sing praises to God, sing praises: sing praises unto our King, sing praises.

Sing ye praises with understanding.

God sitteth upon the throne of his holiness.

The princes of the people are gathered together, even *the people of the God of Abraham: ... he is greatly exalted.*

PSALM 47

Beautiful for situation, the joy of the whole earth, is mount Zion, on the sides of the north, the city of the great King.

God is known in her palaces for a refuge.

We have thought of thy lovingkindness, O God, in the midst of thy temple.

Let mount Zion rejoice, let the daughters of Judah be glad, because of thy judgments.

PSALM 48

My mouth shall speak of wisdom; and the meditation of my heart shall be of understanding.

Man that is in honour, and understandeth not, is like the beasts that perish.

PSALM 49

Out of Zion, the perfection of beauty, God hath shined.

Our God shall come, and shall not keep silence: a fire shall devour before him...

He shall call to the heavens from above, and to the earth...

Gather my saints together unto me; those that have made a covenant with me...

Offer unto God thanksgiving; and pay thy vows unto the most High:

And call upon me in the day of trouble: I will deliver thee, and thou shalt glorify me.

Whoso offereth praise glorifieth me: and to him that ordereth his conversation aright will I shew the salvation of God.

PSALM 50

Wash me throughly from mine iniquity, and cleanse me from my sin.

For I acknowledge my transgressions: and my sin is ever before me.

Behold, thou desirest truth in the inward parts: and in the hidden part *thou shalt make me to know wisdom.*

Purge me with hyssop, and I shall be clean: wash me, and I shall be whiter than snow.

Make me to hear joy and gladness...

Create in me a clean heart, O God; and renew a right spirit within me.

Restore unto me the joy of thy salvation; and uphold me with thy *free spirit.*

Then will I teach transgressors thy ways; and sinners shall be converted unto thee.

PSALM 51

The goodness of God endureth *continually.*

But I am *like a green olive tree in the house of God: I trust in the mercy of God for ever and ever.*

I will praise thee for ever, because thou hast done it: *and I will wait on thy name; for* it is *good before thy saints.*

Psalm 52

$\mathcal{J}\mathcal{O}$

Behold, God is *mine helper: the Lord* is *with them that uphold my soul.*

I will freely sacrifice[20] *unto thee: I will praise thy name, O LORD; for* it is *good.*

Psalm 54

INSIGHT: 20) In the days when the psalms were written, *"sacrifice"* often meant slaughtering a living creature including birds, lambs, rams, bulls; even human sacrifice was practiced. Sacrifice has since come to mean something very different, such as enduring pain and suffering or giving up something one loves or loves to do. However, even in the psalms it is noted that God does not require that kind of sacrifice, but rather the sacrifice of a *"contrite heart,"* in other words, forgiveness, thankfulness, devotion, true humility and especially loving God and one another.

As for me, I will call upon God; and the LORD shall save me.

Evening, and morning, and at noon, will I pray, and cry aloud: and he shall hear my voice.

He hath delivered my soul in peace from the battle that was *against me: for there were many with me.*

Cast thy burden upon the LORD, and he shall sustain thee: he shall never suffer the righteous to be moved.

But I will trust in thee.

PSALM 55

❦

In God will I praise his *word: in the LORD will I praise* his *word.*

In God have I put my trust: I will not be afraid what man can do unto me.

Thy vows are *upon me, O God: I will render praises unto thee.*

...wilt not *thou deliver my feet from falling, that I may walk before God in the light of the living?*

PSALM 56

...my soul trusteth in thee: yea, in the shadow of thy wings will I make my refuge, until these[21] *calamities be overpast.*

God shall send forth his mercy and his truth.

Be thou exalted, O God, above the heavens; let *thy glory* be *above all the earth.*

My heart is fixed, O God, my heart is fixed: I myself *will sing and give praise.*

Awake up, my glory; awake, psaltery and harp: I will awake early.

I will praise thee, O Lord, among the people: I will sing unto thee among the nations.

For thy mercy is *great unto the heavens, and thy truth unto the clouds.*

Be thou exalted, O God, above the heavens: let *thy glory* be *above all the earth.*

PSALM 57

INSIGHT: 21) This verse seems more current without the unitalicized, added word "these." Try re-reading the verse without it.

Because of *his strength will I wait upon thee: for God* is *my defence.*

Let them know that God ruleth in Jacob unto the ends of the earth. Selah.

I will sing of thy power; yea, I will sing aloud of thy mercy in the morning: for thou hast been my defence and refuge in the day of my trouble.

Unto thee, O my strength, will I sing: for God is *my defence,* and *the God of my mercy.*

PSALM 59

Thou hast given a banner to them that fear thee, that it may be displayed because of the truth. Selah.

That thy beloved may be delivered; save with thy right hand, and hear me.

God hath spoken in his holiness; I will rejoice...

Through God we shall do valiantly...

PSALM 60

When my heart is overwhelmed: lead me to the rock that is higher than I.

For thou hast been a shelter for me, and a strong tower from the enemy.

I will abide in thy tabernacle for ever: I will trust in the covert of thy wings. Selah.

Thou hast given me the heritage of those that fear[22] thy name.

So will I sing praise unto thy name for ever, that I may daily perform my vows.

PSALM 61

INSIGHT: 22) Try the word 'honor' in place of 'fear' here = "*...of those that* honor *thy Name.*"

Truly my soul waiteth upon God: from him cometh *my salvation.*

He only is *my rock and my salvation;* he is *my defence; I shall not be greatly moved.*

My soul, wait thou only upon God; for my expectation is *from him.*

In God is *my salvation and my glory: the rock of my strength,* and *my refuge,* is *in God.*

Trust in him at all times; ye people, pour out your heart before him: God is *a refuge for us. Selah.*

Trust not in oppression, and become not vain in robbery: if riches increase, set not your heart upon them.

...power belongeth *unto God.*

Also unto thee, O Lord, belongeth *mercy: for thou renderest to every man according to his work.*

PSALM 62

53

O God, thou art *my God; early will I seek thee: my soul thirsteth for thee, my flesh longeth for thee in a dry and thirsty land, where no water is;*

To see thy power and thy glory, so as *I have seen thee in the sanctuary.*

Because thy lovingkindness is *better than life, my lips shall praise thee.*

Thus will I bless thee while I live: I will lift up my hands in thy name.

My soul shall be satisfied as with *marrow and fatness; and my mouth shall praise* thee *with joyful lips:*

When I remember thee upon my bed, and *meditate on thee in the* night *watches.*

Because thou hast been my help, therefore in the shadow of thy wings will I rejoice.

My soul followeth hard after thee: thy right hand upholdeth me.

Every one that sweareth by him shall glory...

PSALM 63

And all men shall fear, and shall declare the work of God; for they shall wisely consider of his doing.

The righteous shall be glad in the LORD, and shall trust in him; and all the upright in heart shall glory.

PSALM 64

Praise waiteth for thee, O God ... and unto thee shall the vow be performed.

O thou that hearest prayer, unto thee shall all flesh come.

Blessed is the man whom *thou choosest, and causest to approach* unto thee, that *he may dwell in thy courts: we shall be satisfied with the goodness of thy house,* even *of thy holy temple.*

...in righteousness wilt thou answer us, O God of our salvation; who art *the confidence of all the ends of the earth, and of them that are afar off* upon *the sea:*

Which by his strength setteth fast the mountains; being *girded with power:*

Which stilleth the noise of the seas, the noise of their waves, and the tumult of the people.

Thou makest the outgoings of the morning and evening to rejoice.

Thou visitest the earth, and waterest it: thou greatly enrichest it with the river of God, which *is full of water*...

Thou waterest the ridges thereof abundantly: thou settlest the furrows thereof: thou makest it soft with showers: thou blessest the springing thereof.

Thou crownest the year with thy goodness; and thy paths drop fatness.

The little hills rejoice on every side.

The pastures are clothed with flocks; the valleys also are covered over with corn; they shout for joy, they also sing.

PSALM 65

Make a joyful noise unto God, all ye lands:

Sing forth the honour of his name: make his praise glorious.

All the earth shall worship thee, and shall sing unto thee; they shall sing to *thy name. Selah.*

O bless our God, ye people, and make the voice of his praise to be heard:

Which holdeth our soul in life, and suffereth not our feet to be moved.

We went through fire and through water: but thou broughtest us out into a wealthy place.

I will go into thy house with burnt offerings: I will pay thee my vows,

Which my lips have uttered, and my mouth hath spoken, when I was in trouble.

Come and *hear, all ye that fear God, and I will declare what he hath done for my soul.*

If I regard iniquity in my heart, the Lord will not hear me:

But verily God hath heard me; *he hath attended to the voice of my prayer.*

Psalm 66

God be merciful unto us, and bless us; and cause his face to shine upon us; Selah.

That thy way may be known upon earth, thy saving health among all nations.

O let the nations be glad and sing for joy: for thou shalt judge the people righteously, and govern the nations upon earth. Selah.

Let the people praise thee, O God; let all the people praise thee.

Then shall the earth yield her increase; and God, even our own God, shall bless us.

PSALM 67

But let the righteous be glad; let them rejoice before God: yea, let them exceedingly rejoice.

Sing unto God, sing praises to his name: extol him that rideth upon the heavens by his name JAH,[23] *and rejoice before him.*

Thou, O God, didst send a plentiful rain, whereby thou didst confirm thine inheritance, when it was weary.

The Lord gave the word: great was *the company of those that published* it.

The chariots of God are *twenty thousand,* even *thousands of angels: the Lord* is *among them ... in the holy* place.

Blessed be *the Lord,* who *daily loadeth us* with benefits, even *the God of our salvation. Selah.*

INSIGHT: 23) JAH translates as "the sacred name," or "the Lord," per "Strong's Hebrew and Greek Dictionaries."

I will bring my people *again from the depths of the sea:*

They have seen thy goings, O God; even *the goings of my God, my King, in the sanctuary.*

Thy God hath commanded thy strength: strengthen, O God, that which thou hast wrought for us.

To him that rideth upon the heavens of heavens, which were *of old; lo, he doth send out his voice,* and that *a mighty voice.*

Ascribe ye strength unto God: his excellency is *over Israel, and his strength* is *in the clouds.*

O God, thou art *terrible*[24] *out of thy holy places: the God of Israel* is *he that giveth strength and power unto his people. Blessed* be *God.*

INSIGHT: 24) One of the definitions of *"terrible"* in "Strong's" is "morally, to revere." Try reading this portion of the verse as *"O God, thou art* revered *out of thy holy places."*

Let not them that wait on thee, O Lord GOD of hosts, be ashamed for my sake: let not those that seek thee be confounded for my sake, O God of Israel.

But as for me, my prayer is unto thee, O LORD, in an acceptable time: O God, in the multitude of thy mercy hear me, in the truth of thy salvation.

Deliver me out of the mire, and let me not sink...

Hear me, O LORD; for thy lovingkindness is good: turn unto me according to the multitude of thy tender mercies.

And hide not thy face from thy servant; for I am in trouble:

Draw nigh unto my soul, and redeem it:

Let thy salvation, O God, set me up on high.

I will praise the name of God with a song, and will magnify him with thanksgiving.

The humble shall see this, and *be glad: and your heart shall live that seek God.*

Let the heaven and earth praise him, the seas, and every thing that moveth therein.

For God will save Zion ... that they may dwell there, and have it in possession.

...and they that love his name shall dwell therein.

PSALM 69

Let all those that seek thee rejoice and be glad in thee: and let such as love thy salvation say continually, Let God be magnified.

PSALM 70

In thee, O LORD, do I put my trust: let me never be put to confusion.

Let my mouth be filled with thy praise and with thy honour all the day.

But I will hope continually, and will yet praise thee more and more.

My mouth shall shew forth thy righteousness and thy salvation all the day;

I will go in the strength of the Lord GOD...

O God, thou hast taught me from my youth: and hitherto have I declared thy wondrous works.

Now also when I am old and grayheaded, O God, forsake me not; until I have shewed thy strength unto this *generation,* and *thy power to every one* that *is to* come.

Thou, which hast shewed me great and sore troubles, shalt quicken me again, and shalt bring me up again from the depths of the earth.

Thou shalt increase my greatness, and comfort me on every side.

I will also praise thee with the psaltery, even *thy truth, O my God: unto thee will I sing with the harp, O thou Holy One of Israel.*

My lips shall greatly rejoice when I sing unto thee; and my soul, which thou hast redeemed.

PSALM 71

The mountains shall bring peace to the people, and the little hills, by righteousness.

He shall come down like rain upon the mown grass: as showers that water the earth.

In his days shall the righteous flourish; and abundance of peace so long as the moon endureth.

Yea, all kings shall fall down before him: all nations shall serve him.

He shall redeem their soul from deceit and violence: and precious shall their blood be in his sight.

And he shall live, and to him shall be given of the gold of Sheba: prayer also shall be made for him continually; and daily shall he be praised.

His name shall endure for ever: his name shall be continued as long as the sun: and men shall be blessed in him: all nations shall call him blessed.

Blessed be the LORD God, the God of Israel, who only doeth wondrous things.

And blessed be his glorious name for ever: and let the whole earth be filled with his glory; Amen, and Amen.

PSALM 72

...I am continually with thee: thou hast holden me *by my right hand.*

My flesh and my heart faileth: but *God* is *the strength of my heart, and my portion for ever.*

But it is *good for me to draw near to God: I have put my trust in the Lord GOD, that I may declare all thy works.*

PSALM 73

The day is *thine, the night also* is *thine: thou hast prepared the light and the sun.*

Thou hast set all the borders of the earth: thou hast made summer and winter.

O let not the oppressed return ashamed: let the poor and needy praise thy name.

PSALM 74

Unto thee, O God, do we give thanks, unto thee *do we give thanks: for that thy name is near thy wondrous works declare.*

But I will declare for ever; I will sing praises to the God of Jacob.

PSALM 75

In Judah is God known: his name *is great in Israel.*

In Salem[25] *also is his tabernacle, and his dwelling place in Zion.*

PSALM 76

INSIGHT: 25) The word for *"Salem"* can also be translated as 'peaceful' or 'peace.' *"In* peace *also is his tabernacle..."*

I have considered the days of old, the years of ancient times.

I call to remembrance my song in the night: I commune with mine own heart: and my spirit made diligent search.

And I said, This is my infirmity: but I will remember the years of the right hand of the most High.

I will remember the works of the LORD: surely I will remember thy wonders of old.

I will meditate also of all thy work, and talk of thy doings.

Thy way, O God, is in the sanctuary: who is so great a God as our God?

Thou art the God that doest wonders: thou hast declared thy strength among the people.

PSALM 77

Give ear, O my people, to my law: incline your ears to the words of my mouth.

That they might set their hope in God, and not forget the works of God, but keep his commandments:

And they remembered that God was their rock, and the high God their redeemer.

For their heart was not right with him, neither were they stedfast in his covenant.

But made his own people to go forth like sheep, and guided them in the wilderness like a flock.

And he led them on safely, so that they feared not: but the sea overwhelmed their enemies.

And he brought them to the border of his sanctuary, even to this mountain, which his right hand had purchased.

So he fed them according to the integrity of his heart; and guided them by the skilfulness of his hands.

PSALM 78

Help us, O God of our salvation, for the glory of thy name: and deliver us, and purge away our sins, for thy name's sake.

So we thy people and sheep of thy pasture will give thee thanks for ever: we will shew forth thy praise to all generations.

PSALM 79

...thou that dwellest between *the cherubims, shine forth.*

Let thy hand be upon the man of thy right hand, upon the son of man whom *thou madest strong for thyself.*

So will not we go back from thee: quicken us, and we will call upon thy name.

Turn us again, O LORD God of hosts, cause thy face to shine; and we shall be saved.

PSALM 80

Sing aloud unto God our strength: make a joyful noise unto the God of Jacob.

Take a psalm, and bring hither the timbrel, the pleasant harp with the psaltery.

Blow up the trumpet in the new moon, in the time appointed, on our solemn feast day.

Thou calledst in trouble, and I delivered thee; I answered thee in the secret place of thunder:

There shall no strange god be in thee; neither shalt thou worship any strange god.

PSALM 81

Keep not thou silence, O God: hold not thy peace, and be not still, O God.

That men *may know that thou, whose name alone* is *JEHOVAH,*[26] art *the most high over all the earth.*

INSIGHT: 26) *"JEHOVAH"* translates as "the Lord," according to "Strong's." In Exodus 6:3 it is written *"And I appeared unto Abraham, unto Isaac, and unto Jacob, by the name of God Almighty, but by my name JEHOVAH was I not known to them."* Perhaps the *"God Almighty"* referenced there has seemed like a Being mysterious and afar off to people then and now, while the name, JEHOVAH, "the Lord," was perhaps meant to indicate a Being much more accessible and knowable to each of us.

How amiable are *thy tabernacles, O LORD of hosts!*

My soul longeth, yea, even fainteth for the courts of the LORD: my heart and my flesh crieth out for the living God.

Yea, the sparrow hath found an house, and the swallow a nest for herself, where she may lay her young, even thine altars, O LORD of hosts, my King, and my God.

Blessed are *they that dwell in thy house: they will be still praising thee. Selah.*

Blessed is *the man whose strength* is *in thee...*

Who *passing through the valley of Baca*[27] *make it a well; the rain also filleth the pools.*

INSIGHT: 27) "Strong's Hebrew and Greek Dictionaries" define *"Baca"* as "weeping" and "a valley in Palestine," while other references include "a shrub that grows in dry, arid places," reminiscent of the *"valley of the shadow of death"* in Psalm 23 and how the Lord can turn any circumstance into a blessing when it's all yielded to Him.

They go from strength to strength, every one of them in Zion appeareth before God.

Behold, O God our shield, and look upon the face of thine anointed.

For a day in thy courts is better than a thousand. I had rather be a doorkeeper in the house of my God, than to dwell in the tents of wickedness.

For the LORD God is a sun and shield: the LORD will give grace and glory: no good thing will he withhold from them that walk uprightly.

O LORD of hosts, blessed is the man that trusteth in thee.

PSALM 84

Thou hast forgiven the iniquity of thy people, thou hast covered all their sin. Selah.

Thou hast taken away all thy wrath...

Wilt thou not revive us again: that thy people may rejoice in thee?

I will hear what God the LORD will speak: for he will speak peace unto his people, and to his saints: but let them not turn again to folly.

Surely his salvation is nigh them that fear him; that glory may dwell in our land.

Mercy and truth are met together; righteousness and peace have kissed each other.

Truth shall spring out of the earth; and righteousness shall look down from heaven.

Yea, the LORD shall give that which is good; and our land shall yield her increase.

Righteousness shall go before him; and shall set us in the way of his steps.

PSALM 85

His foundation is in the holy mountains.[28]

PSALM 87

INSIGHT: 28) Mountains are the highest physical structures in the natural world, perhaps indicating that our foundations are actually in that which is higher than we are rather than in some primeval slime.

And the heavens shall praise thy wonders, O LORD...

God is greatly to be feared[29] *in the assembly of the saints, and to be had in reverence of all* them that are[30] *about him.*

Thou rulest the raging of the sea: when the waves thereof arise, thou stillest them.

The heavens are *thine, the earth also* is *thine:* as for *the world and the fulness thereof, thou hast founded them.*

Blessed is *the people that know the joyful sound: they shall walk, O LORD, in the light of thy countenance.*

In thy name shall they rejoice all the day: and in thy righteousness shall they be exalted.

But my faithfulness and my mercy shall be *with him: and in my name shall his horn be exalted.*

His seed shall endure for ever, and his throne as the sun before me.

PSALM 89

INSIGHT: 29) 'Respected,' 'honored' or even 'worshiped' would be good alternate interpretations here. 30) Try a second reading of this verse without the unitalicized words.

Lord, thou hast been our dwelling place in all generations.

Before the mountains were brought forth, or ever thou hadst formed the earth and the world, even from everlasting to everlasting, thou art God.

For a thousand years in thy sight are but as yesterday when it is past, and as a watch in the night.

Thou hast set our iniquities before thee, our secret sins in the light of thy countenance.

So teach us to number our days, that we may apply our hearts unto wisdom.

O satisfy us early with thy mercy; that we may rejoice and be glad all our days.

Let thy work appear unto thy servants, and thy glory unto their children.

And let the beauty of the LORD our God be upon us: and establish thou the work of our hands upon us; yea, the work of our hands establish thou it.

PSALM 90

He that dwelleth in the secret place of the most High shall abide under the shadow of the Almighty.

I will say of the LORD, He is my refuge and my fortress: my God; in him will I trust.

Surely he shall deliver thee from the snare of the fowler, and from the noisome pestilence.

He shall cover thee with his feathers, and under his wings shalt thou trust: his truth shall be thy shield and buckler.

Thou shalt not be afraid for the terror by night; nor for the arrow that flieth by day;

Nor for the pestilence that walketh in darkness; nor for the destruction that wasteth at noonday.

Because thou hast made the LORD, which is my refuge, even the most High, thy habitation;

There shall no evil befall thee, neither shall any plague come nigh thy dwelling.

For he shall give his angels charge over thee, to keep thee in all thy ways.

They shall bear thee up in their hands, lest thou dash thy foot against a stone.

Because he hath set his love upon me, therefore will I deliver him: I will set him on high, because he hath known my name.

He shall call upon me, and I will answer him...

With long life will I satisfy him, and shew him my salvation.

PSALM 91

It is a *good* thing *to give thanks unto the LORD, and* to sing praises unto thy name, O most High:

To shew forth thy lovingkindness in the morning, and thy faithfulness every night,

Upon an instrument of ten strings, and upon the psaltery; upon the harp with a solemn sound.

But my horn shalt thou exalt like the horn of *an* unicorn: I shall be anointed with fresh oil.

Those that be planted in the house of the LORD shall flourish in the courts of our God.

They shall still bring forth fruit in old age; they shall be fat and flourishing;

To shew that the LORD is upright: he is *my rock, and* there is *no unrighteousness in him.*

PSALM *92*

82

Thy throne is established of old: thou art *from everlasting.*

The LORD on high is *mightier than the noise of many waters,* yea, than *the mighty waves of the sea.*

Thy testimonies are very sure: holiness becometh thine house, O LORD, for ever.

PSALM 93

Blessed is *the man whom thou chastenest, O LORD, and teachest him out of thy law;*

That thou mayest give him rest from the days of adversity...

For the LORD will not cast off his people, neither will he forsake his inheritance.

But judgment shall return unto righteousness: and all the upright in heart shall follow it.

Unless the LORD had been my help, my soul had almost dwelt in silence.

When I said, My foot slippeth; thy mercy, O LORD, held me up.

In the multitude of my thoughts within me thy comforts delight my soul.

PSALM 94

O come, let us sing unto the LORD: let us make a joyful noise to the rock of our salvation.

Let us come before his presence with thanksgiving...

In his hand are the deep places of the earth: the strength of the hills is his also.

The sea is his, and he made it: and his hands formed the dry land.

O come, let us worship and bow down: let us kneel before the LORD our maker.

For he is our God; and we are the people of his pasture, and the sheep of his hand. To day if ye will hear his voice...

PSALM 95

O worship the LORD in the beauty of holiness: fear before him, all the earth.

Honour and majesty are before him: strength and beauty are in his sanctuary.

Let the heavens rejoice, and let the earth be glad; let the sea roar, and the fulness thereof.

Let the field be joyful, and all that is therein: then shall all the trees of the wood rejoice

Before the LORD: for he cometh, for he cometh to judge the earth: he shall judge the world with righteousness, and the people with his truth.

PSALM 96

Light is sown for the righteous, and gladness for the upright in heart.

PSALM 97

Make a loud noise, and rejoice, and sing praise.

With trumpets and sound of cornet make a joyful noise before the LORD, the King.

PSALM 98

Exalt ye the LORD our God, and worship at his footstool...

Moses and Aaron among his priests, and Samuel among them that call upon his name; they called upon the LORD, and he answered them.

He spake unto them in the cloudy pillar: they kept his testimonies, and the ordinance that *he gave them.*

Thou answeredst them, O LORD our God: thou wast a God that forgavest them...

Exalt the LORD our God, and worship at his holy hill; for the LORD our God is holy.

PSALM 99

Enter into his gates with thanksgiving, and *into his courts with praise: be thankful unto him,* and *bless his name.*

PSALM 100

I will walk within my house with a perfect heart.

I will set no wicked thing before mine eyes...

A froward heart shall depart from me: I will not know a wicked person.

Whoso privily slandereth his neighbour, him will I cut off: him that hath an high look and a proud heart will not I suffer.

Mine eyes shall be *upon the faithful of the land, that they may dwell with me...*

He that worketh deceit shall not dwell within my house: he that telleth lies shall not tarry in my sight.

PSALM 101

Bless the LORD, O my soul: and all that is within me, bless *his holy name.*

Bless the LORD, O my soul, and forget not all his benefits:

Who forgiveth all thine iniquities; who healeth all thy diseases;

Who redeemeth thy life from destruction; who crowneth thee with lovingkindness and tender mercies;

Who satisfieth thy mouth with good things; *so that thy youth is renewed like the eagle's.*

As for *man, his days* are *as grass: as a flower of the field, so he flourisheth.*

Bless the LORD, ye his angels, that excel in strength, that do his commandments, hearkening unto the voice of his word.

Bless ye the LORD, all ye *his hosts; ye ministers of his, that do his pleasure.*

Bless the LORD, all his works in all places of his dominion: bless the LORD, O my soul.

PSALM *103*

Bless the LORD, O my soul. O LORD my God, thou art very great; thou art clothed with honour and majesty.

Who coverest thyself with light as with a garment: who stretchest out the heavens like a curtain:

Who walketh upon the wings of the wind:

Who maketh his angels spirits; his ministers a flaming fire:

He sendeth the springs into the valleys...

They give drink to every beast of the field...

He watereth the hills from his chambers: the earth is satisfied with the fruit of thy works.

He causeth the grass to grow for the cattle, and herb for the service of man: that he may bring forth food out of the earth;

And wine that maketh glad the heart of man, and oil to make his face to shine, and bread which strengtheneth man's heart.

The high hills are a refuge for the wild goats; and the rocks for the conies.

O LORD, how manifold are thy works! in wisdom hast thou made them all: the earth is full of thy riches.

Thou sendest forth thy spirit, they are created: and thou renewest the face of the earth.

The glory of the LORD shall endure for ever: the LORD shall rejoice in his works.

I will sing unto the LORD as long as I live: I will sing praise to my God while I have my being.

My meditation of him shall be sweet: I will be glad in the LORD.

PSALM 104

Glory ye in his holy name: let the heart of them rejoice that seek the LORD.

Seek the LORD, and his strength: seek his face evermore.

Remember his marvellous works that he hath done; his wonders, and the judgments of his mouth...

PSALM 105

✿

Fools because of their transgression, and because of their iniquities, are afflicted.

He sent his word, and healed them, and delivered them from their destructions.

He maketh the storm a calm, so that the waves thereof are still.

Whoso is wise, and will observe these things, even they shall understand the lovingkindness of the LORD.

PSALM 107

O God, my heart is fixed; I will sing and give praise, even with my glory.

Awake, psaltery and harp: I myself will awake early.

Be thou exalted, O God, above the heavens: and thy glory above all the earth;

That thy beloved may be delivered.

Through God we shall do valiantly.

PSALM 108

Thy people shall be willing in the day of thy power, in the beauties of holiness from the womb of the morning: thou hast the dew of thy youth.

Thou art a priest for ever after the order of Melchizedek.

He shall drink of the brook in the way: therefore shall he lift up the head.

PSALM 110

Praise ye the LORD. I will praise the LORD with my *whole heart, in the assembly of the upright, and* in *the congregation.*

The works of the LORD are *great, sought out of all them that have pleasure therein.*

...he will ever be mindful of his covenant.

The works of his hands are *verity and judgment; all his commandments* are *sure.*

He sent redemption unto his people: he hath commanded his covenant for ever: holy and reverend is *his name.*

The fear of the LORD is *the beginning of wisdom: a good understanding have all they that do* his *commandments: his praise endureth for ever.*

PSALM 111

Blessed is *the man* that *feareth the LORD,* that *delighteth greatly in his commandments.*

His seed shall be mighty upon earth...

Wealth and riches shall be *in his house: and his righteousness endureth for ever.*

Unto the upright there ariseth light in the darkness...

A good man sheweth favour, and lendeth: he will guide his affairs with discretion.

He shall not be afraid of evil tidings: his heart is fixed, trusting in the LORD.

His horn shall be exalted with honour.

PSALM 112

Return unto thy rest, O my soul; for the LORD hath dealt bountifully with thee.

For thou hast delivered my soul from death, mine eyes from tears, and *my feet from falling.*

I will walk before the LORD in the land of the living.

PSALM 116

I called upon the LORD in distress:[31] *the LORD answered me,* and set me *in a large place.*

It is *better to trust in the LORD than to put confidence in man.*

It is *better to trust in the LORD than to put confidence in princes.*

The LORD is *my strength and song, and is become my salvation.*

I shall not die, but live, and declare the works of the LORD.

I will praise thee: for thou hast heard me, and art become my salvation.

This is *the day* which *the LORD hath made; we will rejoice and be glad in it.*

Blessed be *he that cometh in the name of the LORD: we have blessed you out of the house of the LORD.*

PSALM *118*

INSIGHT: 31) Distress is interesting in that a person can seldom see beyond it, as if one were enclosed in a very small space, like a closet, where nothing but distress exists. But when one lifts up one's thoughts in consideration of the blessings of the Lord in such case, letting go of the distress in turning to Him, doesn't the weight lift, the walls recede and we are in a much larger and more generous space?

Psalm 119 is considered the longest chapter in the Bible, as well as being the longest acrostic poem, and is my favorite of all the psalms. An acrostic poem is one in which each verse begins with a consecutive letter of the Hebrew alphabet (Aleph, Beth, Gimel, etc.). Psalm 119 is unusual in that it contains 8 verses for each letter in its original (not excerpted) 8-verse form. In Psalm 119, the name of the Hebrew alphabet letter is noted at the beginning of each stanza.   ~ SV

ALEPH.

Blessed are *the undefiled in the way, who walk in the law of the LORD.*

Blessed are *they that keep his testimonies,* and that *seek him with the whole heart.*

They also do no iniquity: they walk in his ways.

O that my ways were directed to keep thy statutes!

Then shall I not be ashamed, when I have respect unto all thy commandments.

I will praise thee with uprightness of heart, when I shall have learned thy righteous judgments.

BETH.

With my whole heart have I sought thee: O let me not wander from thy commandments.

Thy word have I hid in mine heart, that I might not sin against thee.

I will delight myself in thy statutes: I will not forget thy word.

GIMEL.

Open thou mine eyes, that I may behold wondrous things out of thy law.

Remove from me reproach and contempt; for I have kept thy testimonies.

Thy testimonies also are *my delight* and *my Counselors.*

DALETH.

My soul melteth for heaviness: strengthen thou me according unto thy word.

I will run the way of thy commandments, when thou shalt enlarge my heart.

HE.

Incline my heart unto thy testimonies, and not to covetousness.

Turn away mine eyes from beholding vanity; and *quicken thou me in thy way.*

VAU.

I trust in thy word.

And I will walk at liberty: for I seek thy precepts.

And I will delight myself in thy commandments, which I have loved.

And I will meditate in thy statutes.

ZAIN.

I remembered thy judgments of old, O LORD; and have comforted myself.

Thy statutes have been my songs in the house of my pilgrimage.

I have remembered thy name, O LORD, in the night, and have kept thy law.

CHETH.

I intreated thy favour with my whole heart...

I thought on my ways, and turned my feet unto thy testimonies.

At midnight I will rise to give thanks unto thee because of thy righteous judgments.

I am a companion of all them that fear thee, and of them that keep thy precepts.

TETH.

Before I was afflicted I went astray: but now have I kept thy word.

The law of thy mouth is better unto me than thousands of gold and silver.

JOD.

They that fear thee will be glad when they see me; because I have hoped in thy word.

Let thy tender mercies come unto me, that I may live: for thy law is my delight.

Let those that fear thee turn unto me, and those that have known thy testimonies.

Let my heart be sound in thy statutes; that I be not ashamed.

CAPH.

They had almost consumed me upon earth; but I forsook not thy precepts.

Quicken me after thy lovingkindness; so shall I keep the testimony of thy mouth.

LAMED.

For ever, O LORD, thy word is settled in heaven.

They continue this day according to thine ordinances: for all are thy servants.

Unless thy law had been my delights, I should then have perished in mine affliction.

I will never forget thy precepts: for with them thou hast quickened me.

I have seen an end of all perfection: but thy commandment is exceeding broad.

MEM.

O how love I thy law! It is my meditation all the day.

Thy testimonies are *my meditation.*

I understand more than the ancients, because I keep thy precepts.

I have refrained my feet from every evil way, that I might keep thy word.

How sweet are thy words unto my taste! Yea, sweeter than honey to my mouth!

NUN.

Thy word is a lamp unto my feet, and a light unto my path.

I have sworn, and I will perform it, *that I will keep thy righteous judgments.*

My soul is *continually in my hand: yet do I not forget thy law.*

Thy testimonies have I taken as a heritage for ever: for they are *the rejoicing of my heart.*

I have inclined mine heart to perform thy statutes alway, even unto *the end.*

SAMECH.

Depart from me, ye evildoers: for I will keep the commandments of my God.

AIN.

It is *time for* thee, *LORD, to work:* for *they have made void thy law.*

Therefore I love thy commandments above gold; yea, above fine gold.

Therefore I esteem all thy *precepts* concerning *all* things to be *right...*

PE.

Thy testimonies are *wonderful: therefore doth my soul keep them.*

The entrance of thy words giveth light; it giveth understanding unto the simple.

Look thou upon me, and be merciful unto me, as thou usest to do unto those that love thy name.

Order my steps in thy word: and let not any iniquity have dominion over me.

Make thy face to shine upon thy servant; and teach me thy statutes.

TZADDI.

Thy word is *very pure: therefore thy servant loveth it.*

Trouble and anguish have taken hold on me: yet *thy commandments* are *my delights.*

KOPH.

Hear my voice according unto thy lovingkindness: O LORD, quicken me according to thy judgment.

Thou art *near, O LORD; and all thy commandments* are *truth.*

Concerning thy testimonies, I have known of old that thou hast founded them for ever.

RESH.

Consider how I love thy precepts: quicken me, O LORD, according to thy lovingkindness.

Thy word is true from the beginning: and every one of thy righteous judgments endureth for ever.

SCHIN.

My heart standeth in awe of thy word.

Thy law do I love.

Great peace have they which love thy law: and nothing shall offend them.

For all my ways are before thee.

TAU.

Let my supplication come before thee: deliver me according to thy word.

I have longed for thy salvation, O LORD; and thy law is my delight.

END PSALM 119

Deliver my soul, O LORD, from lying lips, and *from a deceitful tongue.*

I will lift up mine eyes unto the hills, from whence cometh my help.

He that keepeth thee will not slumber.

The LORD shall preserve thy going out and thy coming in from this time forth, and even for evermore.

Give thanks unto the name of the LORD.

They shall prosper that love thee.

Peace be within thy walls, and *prosperity within thy palaces.*

Because of the house of the LORD our God I will seek thy good.

Unto thee lift I up mine eyes, O thou that dwellest in the heavens.

PSALM 123

Our soul is escaped as a bird out of the snare of the fowlers: the snare is broken, and we are escaped.

Our help is in the name of the LORD, who made heaven and earth.

PSALM 124

They that trust in the LORD shall be as mount Zion, which cannot be removed, but abideth for ever.

As the mountains are round about Jerusalem, so the LORD is round about his people from henceforth even for ever.

PSALM 125

The LORD hath done great things for us; whereof we are glad.

He that goeth forth and weepeth, bearing precious seed, shall doubtless come again with rejoicing, bringing his sheaves with him.

PSALM *126*

Except the LORD build the house, they labour in vain that build it: except the LORD keep the city, the watchman waketh but *in vain.*

It is *vain for you to rise up early, to sit up late, to eat the bread of sorrows:* for *so he giveth his beloved sleep.*

PSALM *127*

Blessed is *every one that feareth the LORD; that walketh in his ways.*

For thou shalt eat the labour of thine hands: happy shalt *thou* be, *and* it shall be *well with thee.*

Behold, that thus shall the man be blessed that feareth the LORD.

The LORD shall bless thee out of Zion: and thou shalt see the good of Jerusalem all the days of thy life.

PSALM 128

I wait for the LORD, my soul doth wait, and in his word do I hope.

My soul waiteth *for the Lord more than they that watch for the morning:* I say, more than *they that watch for the morning.*

Let Israel hope[32] *in the LORD: for with the LORD* there is *mercy, and with him* is *plenteous redemption.*

And he shall redeem Israel from all his iniquities.

PSALM 130

I have ordained a lamp for mine anointed.

PSALM 132

INSIGHT: 32) As noted previously, try "have confidence" in place of *"hope"* here. *"Let Israel* have confidence *in the Lord..."*

Evening Prayer
(Derived from Psalm 132)

I will not give sleep to mine eyes, or *slumber to mine eyelids,*

Until I find out a place for the LORD...

Arise, O LORD, into thy rest; thou, and the ark of thy strength.

This is *my rest for ever: here will I dwell; for I have desired it.*

O give thanks to the Lord of lords: for his mercy endureth for ever.

PSALM 136

I will praise thee with my whole heart: before the gods will I sing praise unto thee.

Yea, they shall sing in the ways of the LORD: for great is the glory of the LORD.

Though the LORD be high, yet hath he respect unto the lowly: but the proud he knoweth afar off.

PSALM 138

O LORD, thou hast searched me, and known me.

Thou knowest my downsitting and mine uprising, thou understandest my thought afar off.

Thou hast beset me behind and before, and laid thine hand upon me.

Whither shall I go from thy spirit? or whither shall I flee from thy presence?

If I ascend up into heaven, thou art there: if I make my bed in hell, behold, thou art there.

If I take the wings of the morning, and dwell in the uttermost parts of the sea;

Even there shall thy hand lead me, and thy right hand shall hold me.

If I say, Surely the darkness shall cover me; even the night shall be light about me.

Yea, the darkness hideth not from thee...

For thou hast possessed my reins: thou hast covered me in my mother's womb.

I will praise thee; for I am fearfully and wonderfully made: marvellous are thy works; and that my soul knoweth right well.

My substance was not hid from thee, when I was made in secret, and curiously wrought in the lowest parts of the earth.

How precious also are thy thoughts unto me, O God! how great is the sum of them!

Search me, O God, and know my heart: try me, and know my thoughts:

And see if there be any wicked way in me, and lead me in the way everlasting.

PSALM 139

The upright shall dwell in thy presence.

PSALM 140

Let my prayer be set forth before thee as *incense;* and *the lifting up of my hands* as *the evening sacrifice.*

Set a watch, O LORD, before my mouth; keep the door of my lips.

Incline not my heart to any *evil thing, to practise wicked works with men that work iniquity...*

But mine eyes are *unto thee, O GOD the Lord: in thee is my trust; leave not my soul destitute.*

PSALM 141

When my spirit was overwhelmed within me, then thou knewest my path.

I cried unto thee, O LORD: I said, Thou art *my refuge* and *my portion in the land of the living.*

For thou shalt deal bountifully with me.

PSALM 142

In thy faithfulness answer me...

I remember the days of old; I meditate on all thy works; I muse on the work of thy hands.

I stretch forth my hands unto thee: my soul thirsteth *after thee, as a thirsty land. Selah.*

Cause me to hear thy lovingkindness in the morning; for in thee do I trust: cause me to know the way wherein I should walk; for I lift up my soul unto thee.

Teach me to do thy will; for thou art *my God: thy spirit* is *good; lead me into the land of uprightness.*

Quicken me, O LORD, for thy name's sake: for thy righteousness' sake bring my soul out of trouble.

PSALM 143

I will sing a new song unto thee, O God: upon a psaltery and *an instrument of ten strings will I sing praises unto thee.*

Yea, *happy* is that *people, whose God* is *the LORD.*

PSALM 144

I will extol thee, my God, O king; and I will bless thy name for ever and ever.

Every day will I bless thee; and I will praise thy name for ever and ever.

Great is the LORD, and greatly to be praised; and his greatness is unsearchable.

One generation shall praise thy works to another, and shall declare thy mighty acts.

I will speak of the glorious honour of thy majesty, and of thy wondrous works.

They shall abundantly utter the memory of thy great goodness, and shall sing of thy righteousness.

All thy works shall praise thee, O LORD; and thy saints shall bless thee.

The LORD upholdeth all that fall, and raiseth up all those that be bowed down.

The eyes of all wait upon thee; and thou givest them their meat in due season.

Thou openest thine hand, and satisfiest the desire of every living thing.

The LORD is nigh unto all them that call upon him, to all that call upon him in truth.

The LORD preserveth all them that love him...

My mouth shall speak the praise of the LORD: and let all flesh bless his holy name for ever and ever.

PSALM 145

Praise ye the LORD. Praise the LORD, O my soul.

While I live will I praise the LORD: I will sing praises unto my God while I have any being.

Happy is he that hath the God of Jacob for his help, whose hope is in the LORD his God:

The LORD raiseth them that are bowed down: the LORD loveth the righteous:

He relieveth the fatherless and widow...

PSALM *146*

✿

He healeth the broken in heart, and bindeth up their wounds.

He telleth the number of the stars; he calleth them all by their names.

The LORD lifteth up the meek: he casteth the wicked down to the ground.

Sing unto the LORD with thanksgiving; sing praise upon the harp unto our God:

The LORD taketh pleasure in them that fear him, in those that hope in his mercy.

PSALM *147*

Praise ye the LORD from the heavens: praise him in the heights.

Praise ye him, all his angels: praise ye him, all his hosts.

He hath also stablished them for ever and ever: he hath made a decree which shall not pass.

Mountains, and all hills; fruitful trees, and all cedars:

Let them praise the name of the LORD: for his name alone is excellent; his glory is above the earth and heaven.

PSALM 148

Praise ye the LORD. Sing unto the LORD a new song,

Let them praise his name in the dance: let them sing praises unto him with the timbrel and harp.

For the LORD taketh pleasure in his people: he will beautify the meek with salvation.

Let the saints be joyful in glory: let them sing aloud upon their beds.

Let *the high* praises *of God* be *in their mouth, and a twoedged sword in their hand;*

This honour have all his saints. Praise ye the LORD.

PSALM 149

Praise ye the LORD. Praise God in his sanctuary: praise him in the firmament of his power.

Praise him for his mighty acts: praise him according to his excellent greatness.

Praise him with the sound of the trumpet: praise him with the psaltery and harp.

Praise him with the timbrel and dance: praise him with stringed instruments and organs.

Praise him upon the loud cymbals: praise him upon the high sounding cymbals.

Let every thing that hath breath praise the LORD. Praise ye the LORD.

PSALM 150

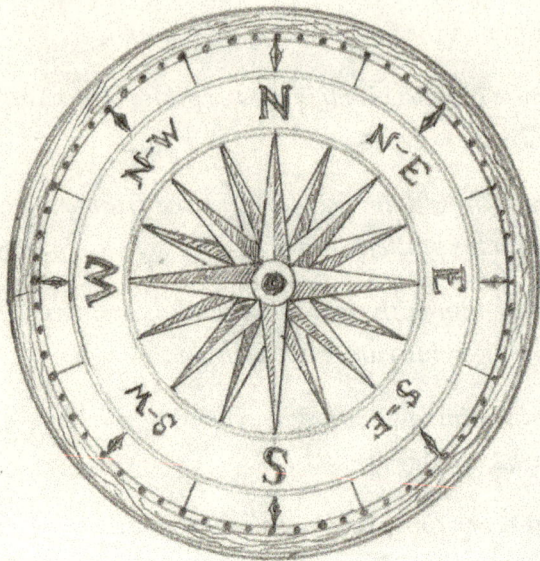

Whither shall I go. . .

INDEX

128

About Dr. Ventola

Dr. Steve Ventola was born on July 5, 1957 in Orange, New Jersey and was raised in West Orange, NJ. He attended Montclair State College (now Montclair University) and graduated with a degree in Health Education. After teaching and coaching High School & Jr. high, Dr. Ventola served as the community health educator, developing and presenting wellness education programs to the populace of West Orange. Through his work in health education, Dr. Ventola was drawn to the healing arts, and in October 1981 moved to Georgia to attend Life Chiropractic College (now Life University). He received his doctor of chiropractic degree in 1985.

Still a practicing chiropractor, health educator and lecturer, Dr. Ventola has been interested in the Bible for some time, and in the Book of Psalms in particular. This interest fueled the creation of the foregoing compilation which he has felt compelled to share with others in the hope that the reader may know the blessings that he has derived from these healing verses.

Dr. Ventola currently makes his home in Atlanta, Georgia.

www.ingramcontent.com/pod-product-compliance
Lightning Source LLC
Chambersburg PA
CBHW030755150426
42813CB00068B/3120/J